HOTEL MAX

Design
Kristen Laina White
kristen@viseblau.com

Art Photography
David May

Printer
The Irwin-Hodson Company
Portland, Oregon
ihco.com

ISBN 0-9644651-3-2
Published by Chetwynd Stapylton
Portland, Oregon
info@chetwynd.com

ART AT THE HOTEL MAX, SEATTLE
Compiled by Tessa Papas

Introduction

I liked the concept. The Max was an old hotel in Seattle that was to be completely revamped in order to show off original artwork and photographs. My assignment was to find local artists and photographers who could produce, within a limited timeframe, around 350 canvases and photographs of sufficient caliber and diversity to enhance the hotel. At that time I knew little of the Seattle art scene so it seemed logical to start my quest in an art school. In May 2004 I met with a group of instructors from Pratt Fine Art Center. They were enthusiastic, word spread and soon I was inundated with an avalanche of imagery. I visited artists' co-ops, studios and homes and came to realize there was a wealth of relatively unknown artistic talent that I could draw on. Later I visited the Photographic Center Northwest and there found I had the choice of much quirky and distinctive imagery by a number of photographers.

Today the Hotel Max, with its pewter-colored guestroom walls and gallery-like corridors, is full of art and photography of such exuberance, color and originality that it can be said a new school is launched, the School of Maximalism! A little tongue in cheek maybe but there are few hotels designed solely for the purpose of displaying original art to the "max"! My heartfelt thanks to all of you who allowed an abstract idea to become a reality, to artists Pam, Jackie, Pirjo, Andrée, Eric, Layne, Tony, Keven, Gretchen, Gail, Evie, Stephanie, Virginia, Gaylen, Howard, Kamla, Zanetka, Moon, Kiki,

MAXIMAL ISM

Jo, Doris, AJ, Bryan, Sharon, Peder, Adele, Amy, Rickie, Junko, and Debbie, and to photographers John, Roniq, Joan, Paul F, Amy, Charles, Zuzana, Erin, Paul S and Lori. I would also like to thank everyone at Ivey Imaging whose persistance found a way to adhere the photographs to the guestroom doors. Many thanks to Pratt Fine Arts Center, to the Photographic Center Northwest and to Atelier 31 for the introductions to artists Adele Sypestyn and Junko Yamamoto. All thanks to the little team in Seattle: Cara King, the design assistant, and David Kennedy, the architect. Finally, a huge thank you to Denise Corso, the designer, who steadfastly believed in her concept and whose creativity and hard work allowed the hotel to become something truly unique.

— Tessa Papas

In a Room Down a Hallway

As a member of that semi-nomadic tribe, the frequent business travelers, I have become inured over the years to standard hotel art reproductions as well as the more recently popular theme hotel room. Grand Rapids French Provincial with Impressionist reproductions giving way in fashion to the more current, mass-market 1940s French Moderne style with its corresponding art no longer elicits more than a qualified nod from me as I unpack my bag and rearrange the desk for work on the road.

The art reproduction on a hotel wall — from historical map and botanical study to the vaguely modernist landscape and tasteful scrap collage — is there to confirm the refinement of the establishment and, in some small way, affirm the social aspirations of the transient occupant. Chosen to complement an existing decorative scheme, the art in hotel rooms is meant to successfully blend into the background, and so it rarely attracts the attention or raises the temperature of the fine arts aficionado.

The Hotel Max has embarked on a more aesthetically complex and potentially engaging solution to the place of

The myriad attitudes and voices evident in the hybrid forms of the artworks provide the rooms with a diverting and unexpectantly entertaining note.

art in the decoration of overnight accommodations. From the lobby to the roof, the Max is filled with original works of art from thirty-nine emerging Seattle artists — works that have been given center stage in the conception of the hotel.

One of the most successful devices in the Max occurs in the hotel's guest-floor hallways, which provide an unexpected, fresh context in which to see a suite of photographs by a single artist. Nine photographers have each been given an entire floor of doorways to showcase their work. Each chose a theme or motif — from intimate images of a couple to images of Seattle's grunge music scene — to explore in photographs large enough to completely cover the guest room doors. Against the dark gray walls and monochromatic carpeting of the hallways, these larger-than-life, black-and-white photographs framed by the doorjambs provide a stunning introduction to the concept of the art-filled hotel and the colorful works that await the guests inside their rooms.

The guest room interiors have been designed to provide a neutral, monochromatic shell in which vibrant commissioned artworks from thirty emerging Seattle artists provide the stimulating frisson of the new, the artists' ideas and handiwork. The myriad attitudes and voices evident in the hybrid forms of the artworks provide the rooms with a diverting and unexpectantly entertaining note. Like Seattle's much-discussed indie music scene of recent years, the range of working styles and differing levels of success evident in the artworks provide an energetic reprise from the formulaic and mundane. While a number of the artists selected for the project are affiliated with Pratt Institute or the Cornish School of Applied Arts, either as faculty or former students, the majority by far are newly emerging and have yet to become widely known beyond Seattle. The variety and vitality of these artists' responses to the décor of hotels and the opportunity to be seen by visitors from around the world reveals much about the current state of the visual arts and how artists are trained today. The showcase provided by the hotel may well be the springboard to wider recognition and acclaim for these artists.

In choosing to commission original photographs, paintings, and collages for all of its guest rooms, the Hotel Max has committed itself to the crucible of this cultural moment, and to the stimulating experience of the work of art, with its invitation to reflect and to question. This adventurous act of cultural patronage suggests new, creative ways to bring serious art into the public's experience and celebrates the plentitude of its practitioners and of aesthetic attitudes at work in Seattle.

BRUCE GUENTHER
PORTLAND ART MUSEUM

Last summer I was on a boat in the waters surrounding the San Juan Islands. It was extremely calm and warm and impossible to see where the waters ended and the sky began. I had wanted to paint water but never had because I was consumed with the idea of "making art" which did not include painting "pictures" of beautiful, breathtaking "scenery"; a "real" artist had the job of redefining art and thus "making a statement." When I returned home, all of those presumptions disappeared; I just wanted to capture the "beauty" of what I had seen on canvas with paint. The San Juan series are my first "water" paintings. I painted from memory and spent many hours trying to understand how water moved, how it reflected light and how it cast its shadow. Painting water has enabled me to use all the knowledge I have amassed over the past three decades about paint, about color and about art. If I have a statement to make it is that I decided not to follow the male model of what art is and what it is supposed to look like. I have come to the conclusion that Clement Greenberg's ideas and ideals concerning value and art have nothing to do with being a woman.

PAM BAKER

I grew up in San Francisco and moved to the Pacific Northwest to attend the University of Oregon in Eugene where I received my BFA in painting. Over the next 20 years, I marched for civil rights, lived on a farm, got married, gave birth to 4 boys, got divorced and in 1996 moved to Seattle to get my MFA in painting. After painting for twenty years and teaching for almost a decade, I dropped out of the art world and recently took on a new career selling software systems. Now, I just paint without concern of making any kind of statement. I am now really enjoying painting because I have finally allowed myself to paint whatever I want. I am completely comfortable referring to myself as a hobbyist. For the first time in my life I am earning good money. Being able to support myself gives me much pleasure. I am healthy and fit, my kids are all well and happy, I earn a good wage, I live on Lake Washington and I am having fun in my studio painting. What more could I ask for?

pam BAKER

opposite page: San Juan III, oil 40 x 30" **this page, from left:**
San Juan II, oil 40 x 30"; San Juan IV, oil 40 x 24"
San Juan V, oil 40 x 24"

My painting, though abstract, has a story to tell. It's meaning is encoded in the language of gesture, color, and line. It is based on visual relationships echoing emotion and thought.

JACKIE BARNETT

I grew up in New York City and went to Vassar College. That was during the fifties when existentialism and abstract expressionism were in our thoughts. My art education began at Stanford University where I worked in the art department with Frank Lobdell and Nathan Oliviera from 1970-1983. It was there that I found my artistic voice and learnt to use my sense of self in the making of art. In Seattle I have had one person shows at the Cliff Michel Gallery, 1989-1993, the Grover Thurston Gallery, 1995-96, and the Foster/White Gallery, 1997-2003. In San Francisco I showed at the Bradford Campbell Gallery and in New York at the Kouros Gallery. Two of my most recent paintings were just selected for the permanent collection of Vassar College.

jackie BARNETT

opposite page: Plié, oil 40 x 30" **this page:**
Chance Encounter, oil 40 x 30"; Enigma oil 40 x 30"

My current body of work investigates the formal and conceptual concerns of painting along with my relationship to painting and interest in process. I have created a methodical way of painting lines and stripes. The work is process-oriented repetition allowing some variation but in the end there is a fluidity of meaning.

ARTIST'S STATEMENT

PIRJO BERG

I was born in Helsinki, Finland, in 1964. At school art and mathematics were my favorite subjects, and when I moved to Seattle in 1991 I fully concentrated on art, mainly in drawing and painting, as well as art philosophy and art history. In 1996 I moved back to Finland to attend the School of Art and Media in Tampere. There I majored in painting but also enjoyed making installations in collaboration with other students. I moved back to Seattle in 2000 and have a studio in Ballard Artists' studio building: Building C. My paintings are inspired by the repetition, texture, lines and the overall feeling of textiles, in particular by the Finnish tradition of making rag rugs and wall hangings. Feminist art theories and practices have also influenced my art making.

pirjo BERG

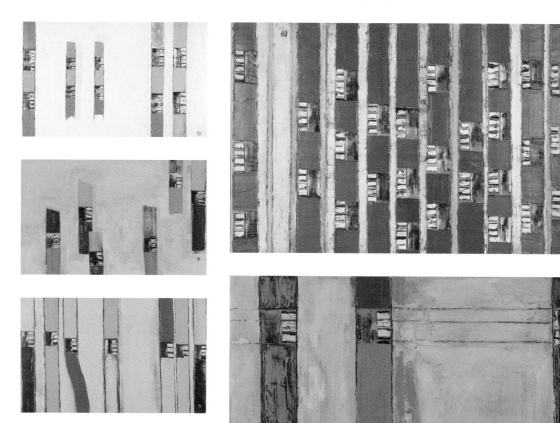

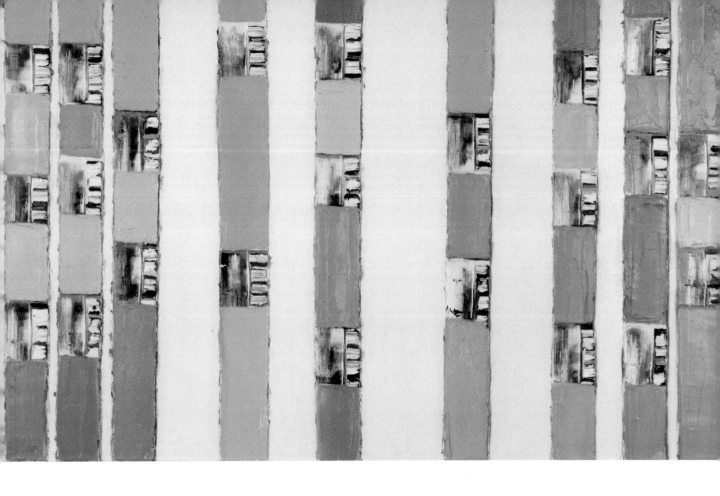

this page: Little Worlds II, oil 40 x 24¨ opposite page, clockwise from left: Little Worlds I, oil 40 x 24¨; Little Worlds III, oil 40 x 24¨ Little Worlds V, oil 40 x 24¨; Little Worlds VI, oil 40 x 24¨; Little Worlds IV, oil 40 x 24¨

I truly enjoy the entire process of black and white photography, from film through chemistry to printing and the magic of the image revealing itself through light and silver. My images are about people and where people have been. Symbols are important to me: symbols of whimsy, aloneness, childhood, sadness and love amongst others.

ARTIST'S STATEMENT

I began working in photography at the age of 5; both of my parents were avid picture takers. I haven't stopped taking pictures since and I have been printing my own work for about twenty years. Some of my photographic heroes: Helen Levitt, Ralph Eugene Meatyard, Mike Disfarmer, Keith Carter, Diane Arbus, Berenice Abbott, Henri Cartier-Bresson and Robert Frank … just to name a few. I began shooting medium format in 1996 and that is my primary camera. I use an old Yashica. All the images from this body of work were shot with this camera. I prefer the old camera, a hand held analog light meter, and I tend to take pictures of objects and people that have an older look. I don't think it's a coincidence.

erin SHAFKIND

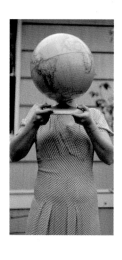

top row, from left: Her head is in the World; Birdcage Dancer; Giraffes and Swings; Songs for the Road
bottom row: Cocktails at the Reception; His Ellipse; Pyramid

2ND FLOOR

top row: In Love; Traveling Love; Two Giraffes; Desert Castle; Holding a Pineapple in Winter
bottom row: Snow Flamingos; Umbrella in the Sun; Traveling Clown; Door to Knowhere; Birdcage and Roses

Color is the dominant force in my paintings because I believe color has the irresistible drawing power of chocolate or opiates. The secondary force is texture because texture brings a sculptural presence that enhances the color. Although color and texture are my focus, I do not plan my palette beforehand nor do I plan the exact types of materials I will use to create a body of work. I use numerous layers of pigment, which reveal and conceal deeper layers through "windows" or "peepholes." These visual metaphors emerge in response to the rhythms of the music that inspire me and from my unconscious taking over during the process of painting. Ultimately, my work uses the potency of color and the physicality of texture to close the gap between viewer and art.

ARTIST'S STATEMENT

ANDREE CARTER

Andrée was born in New Orleans, but now resides in Seattle. In 1992 she graduated cum laude from Loyola University in New Orleans and in 1995 received her MFA from the University of New Orleans. She also studied Renaissance art history in Florence, Italy, in the summer of 1986. Among her major artistic achievements are a painting Fellowship at the Virginia Center for Creative Arts and a recipient of the Percentage for Arts Program in 1997. She was also featured in *New American Paintings* magazine, volume 16 in 1998.

She has had numerous solo exhibitions and has been accepted into several juried exhibitions in Seattle, New Orleans and Berkeley, CA. Andrée is an instructor at the Art Institute of Seattle, Pratt Fine Arts Center and Kirkland Art Center.

andrée CARTER

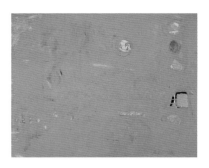

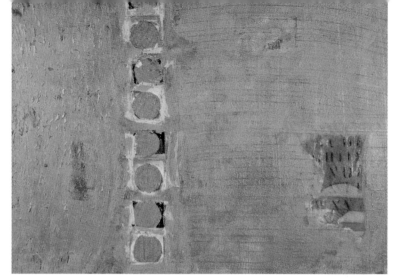

opposite page: Green Stripes, oil 40 x 30"
this page, clockwise from left: Turquoise, oil 40 x 30"
Orange, oil 40 x 30"; Shared Characteristics, oil 40 x 30"
Blue, oil 40 x 30"

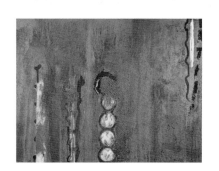

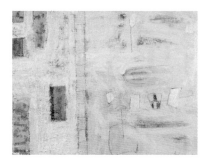

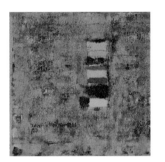

this page, clockwise from left:
Red, oil 30 x 30¨; I didn't want to risk it, oil 40 x 30¨; Of Course, oil 40 x 30¨; Materials and Techniques, oil 30 x 30¨ Much More, oil 30 x 30¨

opposite page, clockwise from left:
Ancient Britons, oil 40 x 30¨ Manning the Office, oil 40 x 24¨ Nobody is Actually Sure, oil 40 x 24¨; Yellow, oil 40 x 30¨; Dark Blue/Fushia Square, oil 40 x 30¨

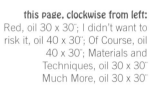

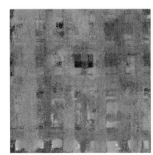

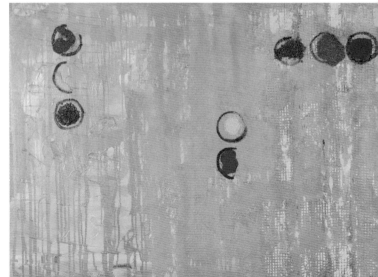

A standard feature in a family car these days is a DVD player. Growing up my DVD player was the rear window of my parents' car. With a constant horizon I would stare out into the changing terrain of arid hills to lush green forest, all within a span of a two-hour drive. Today I continue to be engaged with the landscape and my environment, as I incorporate into my work experiences and memories of places I have been to, am at, and where I would like to go.

ERIC DAY CHAMBERLAIN

Photo:
Michelle Hallen

I grew up in Yakima, Washington, and moved to Seattle nearly twenty years ago. I received a BFA in printmaking from the University of Washington in 1997, and a MFA from Southern Methodist University in 2001. Both schools offered programs outside the usual campus setting. While at UW I spent a quarter in Rome, in the Studio Art program, and at SMU I spent a month in Taos, New Mexico. Both these experiences have been and continue to be influential. I currently teach printmaking and painting at Pratt Fine Art Center in Seattle.

eric CHAMBERLAIN

this page: Untitled III, oil 40 x 24¨ **opposite page, clockwise from left:** Untitled I, oil 40 x 24 in¨; Untitled IV, oil 40 x 30¨; Untitled V, oil 40 x 30¨; Circus, oil 40 x 24¨; Untitled II, oil 40 x 24¨

As an art student in the early 70's, I found that my interest lay in the applied arts. I did some painting, but often was at a loss for subject matter. Now, 30 years later, the ideas flow faster than I can implement them; I like to think that my experience as an older person has contributed to this creative energy. I am fascinated by all aspects of painting: composition, balance of light and shadow and the values of color. I paint a variety of subjects, urban and rural landscapes, figurative, and abstract, and would count among influences Henri Toulouse-Lautrec, Edward Hopper and Richard Diebenkorn. I delight in the process of working on a painting, and hope that some of that joy is conveyed to the viewer through my work.

ARTIST'S STATEMENT

LAYNE COOK

Layne was born in Seattle, Washington, and raised in Portland, Oregon. She moved back to Seattle in 1969 to attend the University of Washington and received a BA degree in art in 1973. In the fall of that year she went to Europe to travel and meet "old world" relatives before settling down to earn a living. She remodeled a number of houses before meeting her husband, a general contractor, and marrying him in 1989. Together they continued remodeling houses while, at the same time, Layne made a living as a kitchen designer in Bellevue, WA. In 2001, she and her husband quit their jobs to take a six-month driving trip around the U.S and Canada. It was during this time that she made the decision to seriously pursue her passion for art. She has been attending workshops and painting daily since then.

layne COOK

opposite page: Call Me Old Fashioned, oil 40 x 30"
this page: Chance Encounter, oil 40 x 24"
Out for the Evening, oil 40 x 24"

The images included in the Vance/Max Hotel remodel are part of a body of work started in 1998 focusing on Buskers/Street Performers and featuring Artis the Spoon Man, Jim Page, Joe Fulton, Tom Frank, Greg Spence-Wolfe and many other regulars of the Seattle and Victoria, B.C. street performance scene. Artis is pleased to have his image included and has fond memories of the years his mother worked at the Vance Hotel. Joan has a high regard for the diverse performers who bring their lively talent to Seattle Pike Place Market.

ARTIST'S STATEMENT

JOAN BROUGHTON

Joan Marian Broughton has enjoyed a lifelong focus on art. A Seattle native and UW art student in the '60s, she has spent time in painting, sculpture, mixed media assemblage and artists' books. Joan began to nurture a serious interest in fine art photography by completing the UW Photography Certificate program in 1999 since followed by ongoing classes and study at the Photographic Center Northwest. She has participated in group exhibitions at the Photographic Center NW including Take My Picture, Paris Student Show and The Passport Series. Joan's day job is in Economic Development, following 25 years as a commercial banker, and she is very committed to her work on the Board of Artist Trust.

joan BROUGHTON

top row, from left: Victoria Buskers; It is polite to tip Scott Free; Emery Carl; Joe Fulton and Shawn McCall; Saturday's Child
bottom row: Greg Spence Wolf; Moonpenny Opera; Ayar; The Gospel Singers

top row: Fiddlin' Jo Fulton; Nan, making history; Magical Tom Frank; Post Alley Juggler; Nightingale
bottom row: Artis; Darth Fiddler; Artis the Spoonman and Jim Page; Juan Rodriquez; Harmonica Man

Tony's artwork deals with ideas based on the concept of communication and ambiguity. It has taken the form of graphs, maps, code and alphabets. In his work he synthesizes ideas based on language and communication into paintings, drawings and digital work that seem both familiar and abstract.

TONY EVANKO

Tony Evanko was born in Albuquerque, New Mexico. He studied painting and drawing in Madrid, Spain, and received a degree in architecture from the University of New Mexico. His artwork has been exhibited in various galleries and museums in the United States and Europe including New York, San Francisco, Sun Valley, Portland, Boston, Germany, and Colombia. He has been invited to lecture and teach special classes and workshops at the University of New Mexico, the Universitario Autonoma de Chihuahua, Mexico, and the Universidad de Antioquia in Medellín, Colombia.

tony EVANKO

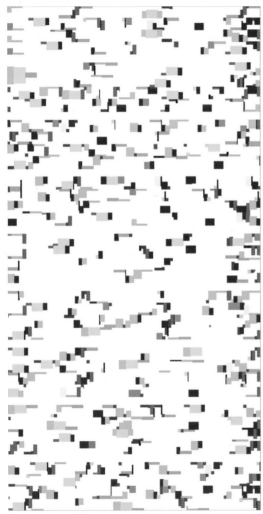

Untitled, mixed media, 55 x 106.5"

KEVEN FURIYA

Born in Indiana, Keven now calls Seattle home. As a child he was encouraged to participate in the arts. However, he focused on science and technology and obtained a Bachelor of Science degree in Mechanical Engineering at Purdue University. Keven spent over 18 years as an engineer but always sketched on the side. This technical background can be seen in his subject matter, which typically involves industrial scenes and cityscapes. In 1995 he studied fine art at Seattle Central Community College and Seattle Fine Art Academy. Keven studied under William E. Elston and became his studio assistant. He has exhibited in various independent venues in Seattle such as Zeitgeist Café/Gallery, Bumbershoot Arts Festival and the Museum of History and Industry. In 2002, Keven was invited to join the Puget Sound Group of Northwest Painters. His influences in style and subject matter include George Bellows, Joaquin Sorolla and John Singer Sargent.

I like to paint because I enjoy it and its fun. 'Nuff said.

keven FURIYA

When offered a commission to paint for a hotel, I took it. When I was asked if I could make some "abstract/figurative" paintings, I said of course. Then I got off the phone and realized I had no idea what that meant or where to start. These paintings are the result of integrating my figurative work with my abstract. I lost the heads and traded in complete ambiguity for a little more structure. The result reminds me of women as landscapes. I love the shapes of limbs. I love the simplicity of graphite line work. I love color. I took the curves and solidity of female forms and used them as a foundation for intricate scribblings, fake mountains, sexy towers, and bumpy horizons. I feel the work ended with emotion to tell a story, yet with vague oddities to simply feast your eyes upon.

ARTIST'S STATEMENT

GRETCHEN GAMMELL

Gretchen Gammell graduated with a degree in painting from Oregon College of Arts and Crafts. She has exhibited her watercolors and figurative work for the past five years at the Attic Gallery in Portland and is also represented by the Winsor Gallery in Vancouver, BC. Gretchen continues to take commissions from previous clients and new businesses while pursuing representation with new galleries. Her work remains rooted in the exploration of the female form and mind while balancing personal issues such as the pleasure and intrigue she finds through the unusual colors and marks of her abstract style.

gretchen GAMMELL

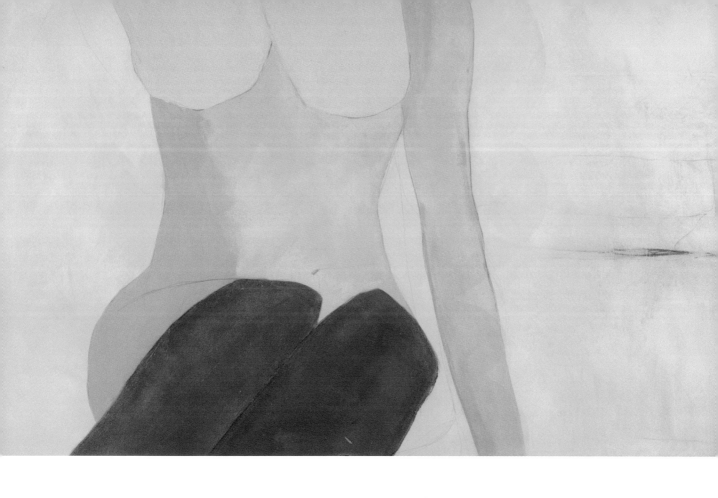

this page: Red Stockings, acrylic 40 x 24¨ **opposite page, clockwise from left:** Green/yellow/blue, acrylic 40 x 24¨; Yellow Camisole, acrylic 40 x 24¨ Green/pink, acrylic 40 x 24¨; Pink Lady, acrylic 40 x 24¨; Blue Torso, acrylic 40 x 24¨

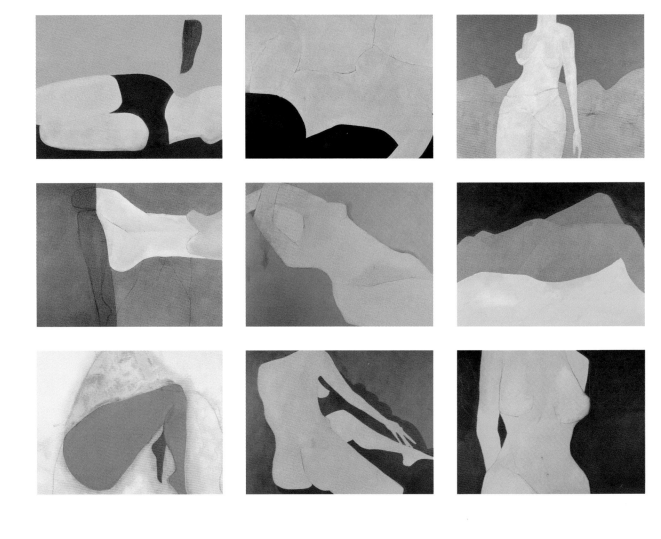

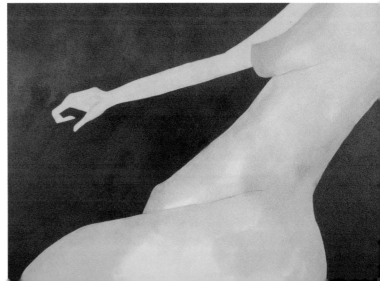

this page, right: Lilac Nude, acrylic 40 x 30"; Come Hither, acrylic 40 x 30" above: Brown Skirt, acrylic 30 x 40"
opposite page, top row, from left: Pink/yellow, acrylic 40 x 30" Orange/purple, acrylic 40 x 30"; Yellow Nude, acrylic 40 x 30"
middle row: Yellow Torso, acrylic 40 x 30"; Orange Nude, acrylic 40 x 30"; Red Nude, acrylic 40 x 30" bottom row: Purple Stockings, acrylic 40 x 30"; Arched Foot, acrylic 40 x 30"; Green Torso, acrylic 40 x 30"

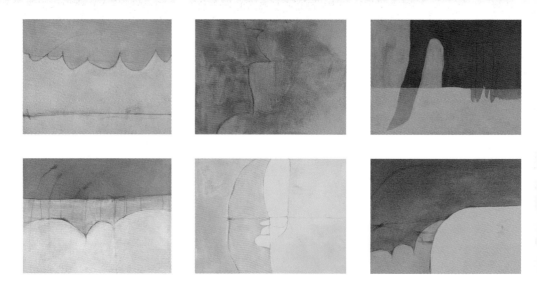

from top left: Orange/tangerine, acrylic 16 x 12¨; Red/gray, acrylic16 x 12¨; Red/pink, acrylic 16 x 12¨
Yellow/pink, acrylic 16 x 12¨; Green/yellow, acrylic16 x 12¨; Red/orange, acrylic 16 x 12¨

PAUL SUNDBERG

Paul Sundberg is a photographer and teacher from Seattle. His photography is constructed on narrative themes and the spontaneity of street photography.

paul SUNDBERG

top row, from left: Girl at fountain; Mika at the beach; Hoops; Kitchen window; Anna
bottom row: P.I.; Seven; Mr. Schmidt #1; Juggler

4TH FLOOR

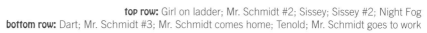

top row: Girl on ladder; Mr. Schmidt #2; Sissey; Sissey #2; Night Fog
bottom row: Dart; Mr. Schmidt #3; Mr. Schmidt comes home; Tenold; Mr. Schmidt goes to work

My work is a response to my own life – much like visual journal keeping. I utilize both the things I have control over and circumstances that are not of my own making. I tend to think of this work as an expression of my understanding of a place that exists between nature and culture. The work looks as it does at any given time because I change or adapt materials, work methods, size and format depending on my physical environment and what materials are available to me in the current situation.

ARTIST'S STATEMENT

GAIL GRINNELL

Photo:
Hannah Wildman

Gail Grinnell was born in Richland and studied at the University of Washington (B.F.A., 1988). Among innumerable honors she has been an Artist in Residence at the Centrum Foundation (Port Townsend, WA, 1990, 1993) and Pratt Fine Arts Center (Seattle, WA, 1996/97). Her work has been exhibited in many regional venues, among them the Art Museum of Missoula, (1996) and Maturango Museum, Ridgecrest, CA (1998). She is represented by the Francine Seders Gallery, Seattle, and her work has been included in many group exhibitions, most recently 4x4: Four Artist/Four Decades of School of Art Alumni at the University of Washington, Seattle, in 2000, South meets North, Instituto de Artes Graficas de Oaxaca, Mexico, and at the Shenzhen Art Institute, Shenzhen, China (2005). Her work is in many collections in and around Seattle and Tacoma.

gail GRINNELL

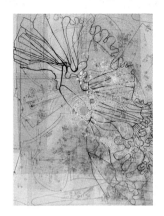 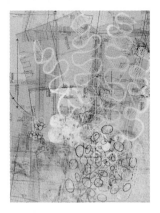

from left: Pleat, oil 30 x 40¨; Fold, oil 30 x 40¨; Gather, oil 30 x 40¨

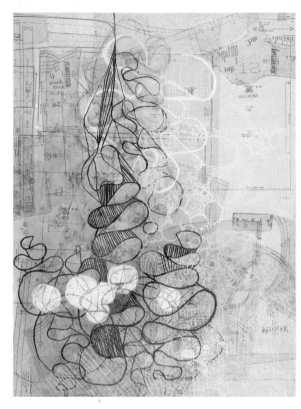

EVY HALVORSEN

I was born in Norway but brought up in Seattle and in our home in Ballard was a painting above the fireplace that my grandfather had created after he retired. It was a painting of the area that I was born in. I have no real memories of him but I spent a lot of time looking at that image. I also wanted to be able to create work that would live on after me and reflect something of my life and interests. As a teen-ager my early artistic influences were Paul Klee and Van Gogh. I was strongly attracted to them because of their sense of color, play and the emotion conveyed in that bold use of color. Studying at Cornish, so many years later, color was still important in my work and has played a significant role in my painting and printmaking since then.

What I'm looking for could be best described as a welcoming space, a place to be drawn into. It is geographical but pulled to the extremes between inner and distant space, tempered by time and memory. "The contradiction so puzzling to the ordinary way of thinking comes from the fact that we have to use language to communicate our inner experience, which in its very nature transcends linguistics." D.T. Suzuki

evy HALVORSEN

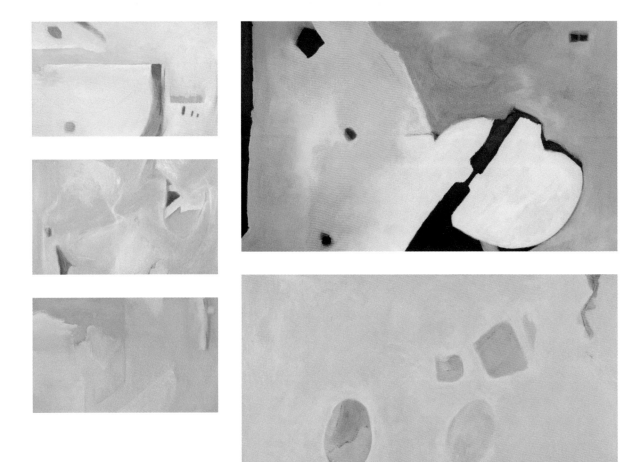

this page: Betwixt, oil 40 x 24¨ **opposite page, clockwise from left:** Light Rise, oil 40 x 24¨; Arriving, oil 40 x 24¨; Drifting Away, oil 40 x 24¨
Tilted Memory, oil 40 x 24¨; April Confusion, oil 40 x 24¨

My paintings are rooted in organic forms and influenced by the architecture of natural structures. The correlation between this imagery and my use of earth-derived components is intentional. I love line, texture and saturated color. I try to create work that has a design element but also looks 'grown.'

I'm captivated by bee's wax — the way it looks, feels, and the way it smells. I find it inherently lovely, but also a tad bit 'eerie'. It is transparent — possesses movement, depth and versatility. Having a background in clay, I feel attracted to its viscosity — it can be carved, melted and really handled. It's so physical. I cannot hear music without seeing colors, texture, movement and images. For me, encaustic paintings are layered like music. They can be rich, 'loud', or clear, subtle and 'quiet', but never one-dimensional.

My influences are my favorite musicians and visual artists: Cézanne, Matisse, Kahlo, Juan Alonso, Fay Jones, Debra Mersky, John Grade, Terry Terrell, Rachel Illingworth, PJ Harvey, and Billie Holiday. I have been inspired and amazed by each of them in different ways.

stephanie HARGRAVE

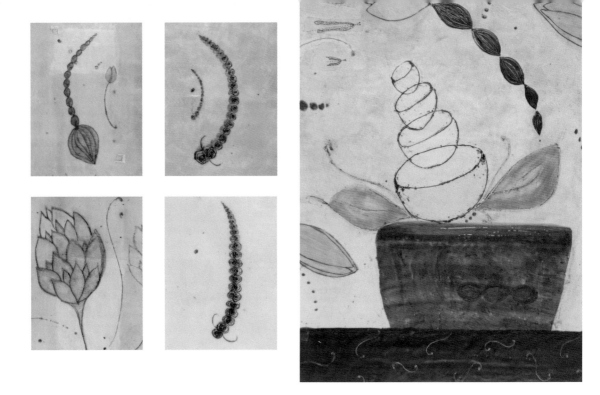

OPPOSITE PAGE, CLOCKWISE FROM LEFT: Lily, encaustic 30 x 40˝; Flora, encaustic 30 x 40˝;
Lotus & Spiro, encaustic 16 x 12˝; Bowls, encaustic 16 x 12˝; Pods, encaustic 16 x 12˝
THIS PAGE, CLOCKWISE FROM LEFT: Pale Spike Bird, encaustic 12 x 16˝; Savim II, encaustic 12 x 16˝; Spring, encaustic 30 x 40˝;
Centipede II, encaustic 12 x 16˝; Pale Artichoke Bloom, encaustic 12 x 16˝

CHARLES PETERSON

Photo:
Mascha Kroenlein

Born in 1964, Peterson is best known for his documentation of the music phenomenon known as "grunge", culminating in the critically acclaimed monograph *Touch Me I'm Sick* (powerHouse, 2003). Peterson's photographs have graced hundreds of record covers, and appeared in publications worldwide including the *Village Voice, NME, The New York Times, Mojo, People, Rolling Stone, Spin, Entertainment Weekly, The Independent, Guitar World,* and *Newsweek,* as well as numerous other media on the Seattle music scene. He has two previous monographs, *Screaming Life* (Harper Collins, 1995) and *Pearl Jam: Place/Date* (with Lance Mercer, Rizzoli/Vitalogy, 1997). In the spring of 2005 he had his first major exhibition at the Chrysler Museum of Art in Norfolk, Virginia, and his photographs are featured in the permanent collection of Seattle's Experience Music Project (EMP). He is also with Getty Images and Retna Ltd. Peterson lives in Seattle with his dog Barkley and is working on a book of his travels to Vietnam.

charles PETERSON

top row, from left: Pearl Jam, Seattle, 1992; Endfest, Kitsap County Fairgrounds, WA 1991; Laughing Hyenas, Seattle, 1991 Nirvana, Los Angeles, 1990; L7, Los Angeles, 1990 **bottom row:** Pearl Jam, Spain, 1996; Nirvana, Los Angeles, 1990 Soundgarden, Berkeley, CA 1989; Nirvana, Seattle, 1990

5TH FLOOR

top row: Pearl Jam, Oakland, CA 1997; Big Black, Seattle, 1995; Nirvana, Reading, UK, 1992; Hole, Seattle, 1992
Fugazi, Olympia, WA, 1991 **bottom row:** Mudhoney, Seattle, 1989; Pearl Jam, Budapest, 1996; Nirvana, Seattle, 1990
Pearl Jam, Barcelona, 1996; Endfest, Kitsap County Fairgrounds, WA, 1991

Skies are a universal daily experience. The color, light and movement of the sky are an intrinsic part of our connection to the natural landscape. I group pieces of sky - juxtaposing days, times, and qualities of light to create glimpses of memory and reflection.

VIRGINIA HOWLETT

Canadian artist Virginia Howlett holds a BFA from Ohio State University and an MFA in Painting from the Art Institute of Chicago. She was an Assistant Professor at Hampton University in Virginia where she won a Mellon Foundation grant for painting in Oaxaca, Mexico. She was also an Assistant Professor of Painting at New Mexico Highlands University, near Santa Fé. Virginia moved to Seattle and fell in love with the Pacific Northwest landscape. She creates her work at an island cabin in British Columbia, in the Sonoran desert of Arizona, and at her Ballard studio. Her exhibitions include shows in Seattle, New Mexico, Hampton, Virginia, Columbus, Ohio and Chicago.

virginia HOWLETT

A friend once called my painting a "muscleman painting" because he could see by looking at it how I had physically fought with it to get it where I wanted. My work is about process, human emotion and struggle.

GAYLEN IWASAKI

Born and raised in Seattle I grew up very shy. I can remember spending hours alone as a child drawing but It wasn't until I was in my mid thirties that I started painting and committed myself to art. Although not formally trained I've had great mentors. Drake Deknatel has been a great inspiration as well as a friend. Over the years I have been particularly influenced by the works of de Kooning, Guston, Kokoschka, Beckmann and Baslitz. Some of my achievements have been a residency at Vermont Studio Center and Pathway Scholarship/ Pratt Fine Art Center. Paintings are in the collection of the Seattle Center and Pure Image to name a few. My work is currently available at the Seattle Art Museum Rental Sales Gallery.

gaylen IWASAKI

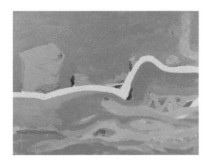

opposite page: Flight, mixed media 40 x 30"
this page, clockwise from left: Panic, oil 40 x 30"
Not from Here, mixed media 40 x 30"; Blind Date, mixed
media 40 x 30"; Visitors, mixed media 40 x 30"

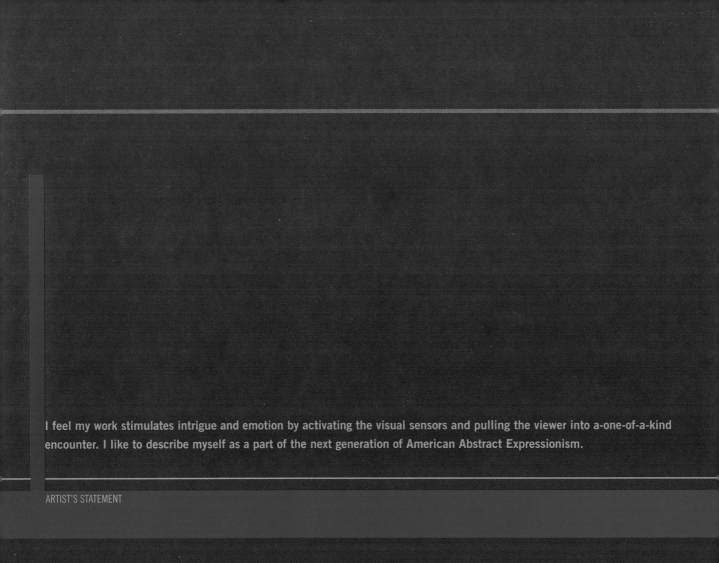

I feel my work stimulates intrigue and emotion by activating the visual sensors and pulling the viewer into a-one-of-a-kind encounter. I like to describe myself as a part of the next generation of American Abstract Expressionism.

ARTIST'S STATEMENT

HOWARD JACOBS

Howard grew up in southern California and graduated from the University of Nevada in Las Vegas. He slowly worked his way north and has now lived in the Northwest for the past six years. His work explores boldly colored non-representational forms and utilizes a broad range of materials and mediums, among them oil-based enamel, traditional oil paint, metal, glass, rope, nails and sand. His approach in the creation of such art mirrors that of Jackson Pollock. Each painting is produced directly on the ground in an unorthodox physical effort with the paint and some have exceeded twelve feet in length. Many have likened his work with that of Gerhard Richter and Lee Krasner. His work is in many private collections across the country.

howard JACOBS

Impact of War, oil 30 x 48"

ZUZANA SADKOVA

Coming from the Czech Republic to the United States, Zuzana Sadkova brings to her fine art photography a joint sensibility of European and American influences. This young artist's work began with architectural portraits in the mid-90s, and continues through her formal education at Seattle's Photographic Center Northwest where she is now completing her thesis. Sadkova's work draws from the inspiration of her native Josef Sudek and local visionary Imogen Cunningham. Her fine art photography has been shown in several cities including Prague and Seattle, and her documentary work has been commissioned by international aid organizations, and was presented at the American Anthropological Association National Convention in Chicago in 2003. Sadkova has lectured on visual anthropology in Beijing, and has received a national award for her black and white photographs in the Czech Republic.

The timeless charm of European architecture speaks through this collection as I try to capture moments of grand human expression. One can find them in the corners, passages and edifices of the masters. It is an honor to have my impressions join the permanent collection of the historic Vance/Max Hotel.

ARTIST'S STATEMENT

zuzana SADKOVA

top row, from left: Paris, 2002; New York City, 2000; Český Krumlov, 1999
bottom row: New York City, 2000; Prague, 1999; Amsterdam, 2001

top row: Paris, 2002; New York City, 2000; New York City, 2000; Paris, 2000; Paris, 2000
bottom row: New York City, 2000; Oxford, 2000; Oxford, 2000; Kutná Hora, 2002; Křišťanov, 2002

Art making began for me with oil painting. After some time the process of oil painting became tedious and the way I was working didn't allow for play. Then I discovered printmaking as a medium. For years I appreciated the serendipitous nature of the process of monoprinting. I enjoyed layering color and meaning but in time I found that I wanted more control over my mark making. I didn't need the chance happenings that kept me interested in printmaking anymore. I returned to painting this time with beeswax and oil. I am still layering colors but am able to physically build a surface up from the substrate. I work in series often on more than one piece at a time. I am more interested in the process of making than in the end product itself.

ARTIST'S STATEMENT

KAMLA KAKARIA

Kamla Kakaria received her MFA from the University of Washington in 2000. She currently manages the Printmaking/2D department at Pratt Fine Arts Center. She also teaches at KAC and NSCC. Kamla has shown in and around the Seattle area and internationally in Mexico. She has had various residencies and her work is in many collections including the University of Washington, Safeco Corporation and Vulcan Incorporated. Kamla's work can be seen at the Seattle Art Museum's Rental Sales Gallery.

kamla KAKARIA

top row, from left: Little Dress #1, encaustic 12 x 16¨.; Little Dress #2, encaustic 12 x 16¨; Little Dress #3, encaustic 12 x 16¨; Little Dress #4, encaustic 12 x 16¨; Little Dress #5, encaustic 12 x 16¨ **middle row:** Passing Through III, encaustic 12 x 16¨; Passing Through II, encaustic 12 x 16¨ Passing Through I, encaustic 16 x 12¨; Passing Through IV, encaustic 16 x 12¨ **bottom row:** Passing Through V, encaustic 16 x 12¨ Passing Through VI, encaustic 16 x 12¨

ZANETKA KRAL (KRALOVA GAWRONSKI)

My family and I immigrated to the USA from Slovakia when I was very young. This dramatic change influenced my perception of the world and led me to pursue a life dedicated to the arts. I have been painting for more than eighteen years and received my formal training from the Pennsylvania Academy of Fine Arts, Philadelphia. My involvement in the arts has spanned a broad spectrum: theatrical set designs, children's museum exhibit designs and fabrication, book cover illustration, murals, fabrication team for the Nickelodeon Network Blues Clues, TV Land and the Big Help Mobile, instructor at the Art Institute of Seattle. In addition to commissioned paintings and sculptures, I exhibit my work nationally. Currently, I live in Seattle with my husband and three cats and enjoy spending my free time rock climbing, skiing and sea kayaking.

I am interested in what is often overlooked, yet with a second glance is revealed to be precious. There are moments in a day that quietly slip by without notice, the time in-between memories, this is what I am interested in. This is what I paint.

zanetka KRAL

this page: Quiet Expectations, oil 40 x 24¨

opposite page, clockwise from left: Evidence of the Carving Wind, oil 40 x 30¨; Wedding, oil 40 x 30¨; The Egg Collector, oil 40 x 30¨
If the Past Could Speak Again, oil 40 x 30¨; The Warm Edge of Celebration, oil 40 x 30¨

top row, from left: Timeless Season, oil 24 x 40"; Lemons, oil 16 x 12"; Quiet, oil 16 x 12"
middle row: Secret Places, oil 40 x 24"; Discovery, oil 16 x 12"; Duck Book, oil 16 x 12"
bottom row: Riding Home, oil 16 x 12"; Late Summer, oil 16 x 12"

clockwise from left: Anticipation, oil 40 x 30"; Long Awaited Dream, oil 40 x 30"; Held by the Wind, oil 40 x 30"; Three Saints, oil 40 x 30"

I like to explore human relationships, the bonds between individuals and the beliefs and values that govern our daily interactions intrigue me. I hope these works address ideas that go beyond social and cultural lines, and include humanistic ties and personal connections. However, as we are all social beings, we are also bound to forces that are greater than ourselves. The characters in my pieces are people from my own life because I find inspiration and perspective in them. The texture and form of my work varies depending upon the environment in which the characters are envisioned. I work with different materials such as ink gel pens, sumi ink and rice paper to convey the message in my work.

ARTIST'S STATEMENT

MOON LEE

Moon Lee was born into a comfortable middle class family in Seoul, South Korea. She attended the Hong Ik University there and obtained a BFA in oriental painting in 1976.

A couple of years later she was married to a Korean businessman. This was an arranged marriage with a man she hardly knew and after two children the relationship turned abusive. Moon had already moved to Seattle and after her divorce in 1992 she enrolled at Cornish College of Art to study printmaking. On completing her studies she changed her artistic focus to studying the importance of human relationships and their many dimensions. Today, Moon continues to paint and to teach from her studio in Bellevue.

LEE
moon

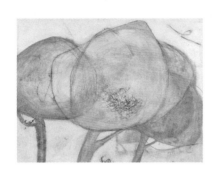

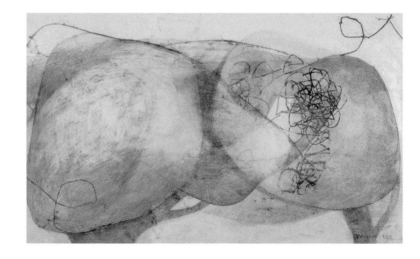

this page: Relationship III, mixed media 40 x 24" **opposite page, from left:** Relationship I, mixed media 40 x 30";
Relationship II, mixed media 40 x 24"; Relationship IV, mixed media 40 x 24"

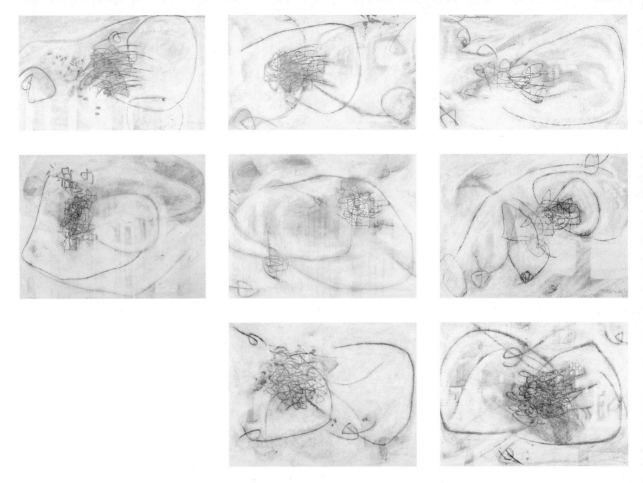

top row, from left: My Eden I, mixed media 40 x 24¨; My Eden IV, mixed media 40 x 24¨; Serendipity III, mixed media 40 x 24¨;
middle row: My Eden II, mixed media 40 x 30¨.; My Eden III, mixed media 40 x 30¨; Serendipity I, mixed media 40 x 30¨
bottom row: Serendipity II, mixed media 40 x 30¨; Neighborhood Watch, mixed media 40 x 30¨

RONIQ BARTENEN

I was born in Ashland, Oregon, and, with stops along the west coast, landed in Seattle in 1986. My love of photography has steadily evolved over the years, leading me to be involved in several group shows as well as solo exhibitions. I have been published in the book *Chasing Dreams,* worked on a commercial project for a hotel locally, and was featured with other female photographers in the Northwest Women's Photography exhibit at the Washington State Convention and Trade Center. I have also been involved in several Paris photography exhibits as well as a juried show through the Photographic Center Northwest.

My love of travel has taken me to some incredible places. Sharpening my photographic eye, broadening my mind and exposing myself to new cultures have left me wanting to see as much of the world as I can. I love to capture bits of life and time. Sometimes surreal, sometimes just as they are for that one moment and letting my eyes take it all in with every adventure, I'm open to new ways of seeing the world around me.

ARTIST'S STATEMENT

roniq BARTENEN

top row, from left: Courtyard, Paris; Musée d'Orsay, Paris; Gate, Prague; Cutlery Shop, Spain; Musée d'Orsay, Paris
bottom row: Tree & Tower, Prague; Liberty Island, New York; Two Geese, Spain; Time, New York

7TH FLOOR

top row: Luxembourg Gardens Paris; Swan, France; Jardin, Paris; Parc St. Cloud, France; Bath Abbey, England
bottom row: Broken Foot, Spain; Marché aux Puces de Saint Ouen, Paris; Statue, Ireland; Mannequin, Paris; Cemetary, Paris

About Swimmers: Figures depicted in water are a recurrent theme in my work. I swim regularly and think about the two realities inside and outside the water while swimming. My paintings address the pleasure of being in water as well as the distinctly altered reality that exists under water.

KIKI MACINNIS

Kiki MacInnis received her MFA in painting from the Otis College of Art and Design in Los Angeles. She teaches drawing at Pratt Fine Art Center in Seattle. In 2004 Kiki spent three weeks as an Artist Resident at Centrum in Port Townsend, Washington. The brush and ink drawings of organic matter produced during the residency were shown at the Kirkland Art Center in July and August of 2004 in a show titled "Shore Lines." The brushwork shapes displayed in the figurative work here derive from the studies of organic shapes in black ink.

kiki MACINNIS

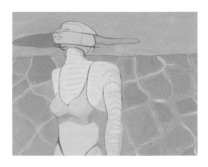
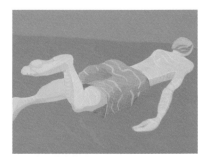
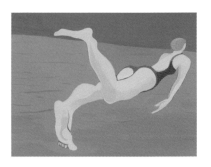

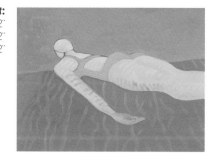

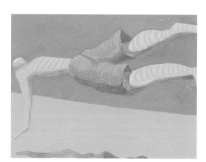

The evolution of my painting has been a swing from the abstract to nearly expressionistic and back to the abstract. At present I am interested in devolving the landscape into more soft sculptural expressions. This is my secondary objective as an architect and becomes focal as the primary goal of my artist self. I create with an eye toward subtle visual impact and contact with the viewer in a personal way.

JO MONIZ, AIA

Jo Moniz is a practicing architect in Seattle, Washington. She received her Bachelor of Arts in Environmental Design from the University of Washington in 1977 and her Washington State architectural license in 1984. Her art education began at Southern Oregon University where she studied all major media as well as art history. Jo has returned to art in recent years studying primarily oil painting while continuing her private architectural practice. The design of her private residence was published in *Arcade Magazine* in an article titled "Wood: Use and Meaning" in 1984. Her focus for future pieces is to further explore oil and mixed media in a large format incorporating loose geometry and organic abstract shapes. Art influences have been Robert Natkin, Richard Diebenkorn, Mark Rothko and Paul Klee.

*jo*MONIZ

this page:
Sequim Hill & Sky, oil crayon 16 x 12"
Ebey Hill & Lake, oil crayon 16 x 12"

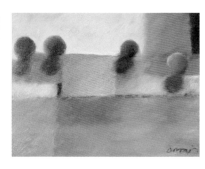

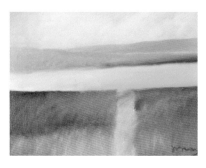

top row, from left:
Madras Hill & Lake, oil crayon
12 x 16¨; Columbia River & Hill,
oil crayon 12 x 16¨; Palouse Hill
& Moon, oil crayon 12 x 16¨
bottom row: Palouse Hills Sky, oil
crayon 12 x 16¨; Methow Hill &
Sky, oil crayon 12 x 16¨
Widbey Hill & Sky, oil crayon
12 x 16¨

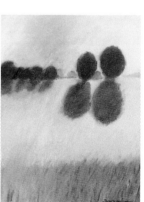

Rich color, unique forms and layered textures continue to draw me into collage experiments. I am influenced by antique textiles and their patterns, colors and designs that reflect natural shapes. Collage and overprinting allow me to combine abstract elements with images from nature. Playing along the edge of what is 'given' and what is unknown presents a unique space of openness, curiosity about outcome, and finally satisfaction that is, for me, rarely found in such potent and pleasurable form anywhere else in life.

ARTIST'S STATEMENT

DORIS MOSLER

Doris Mosler is a self-taught artist with a background in design and a love of texture and pattern. After ten years in advertising and design she decided a freelance creative career would be both more challenging and satisfying and offer the sense of freedom she so enjoys. After extensive travels in Europe, Turkey, India, Nepal and Tibet and then attendance at workshops in monotype she found a formula to convey the visual imagery, art history and textiles of the countries she had visited. Monotype, she felt, was a medium that offered the versatility and spontaneity she loved as well as satisfying her inner sense of adventure. Doris is currently a monotype instructor at Pratt Fine Arts Center and at her studio in Seattle. Her work is in a number of collections in the Northwest and abroad and she is represented by the Seattle Art Museum Rental Sales Gallery and the San Francisco-based art publisher ImageConscious.

doris MOSLER

this page: Mixed Media #3, 40 x 24˝ opposite page: Mixed Media #1, 40 x 30˝; Mixed Media #2, 40 x 30˝

Take one fresh and tender kiss
Add one stolen night of bliss
One girl, one boy
Some grief, some joy
Memories are made of this

as recorded by Dean Martin and the Easy Riders

AMY MULLEN

Amy Mullen was born and raised in Poulsbo, WA. She graduated from North Kitsap High School in 1996 where she took her very first photography course. She continued her photography education at Edmonds Community College and was also founder and president of the school's first photography club. Upon receiving her Associates of Arts degree, she transferred to PCNW to pursue a Certificate of Photography. In June 2004, Amy graduated from PCNW in Seattle displaying her capstone project "Mirrors," a culmination of her 5 year program. Amy specializes in black and white fine art photography. Her images have been featured in "Beneath the Surface" at the Photographic Center Northwest (PCNW) gallery in August 2001, a competition exhibition juried by Magnum member Chien-Chi Chang, and "Celebrating Women in the Arts" sponsored by the Frye Art Museum in January 2003, a juried exhibition highlighting photographs of Contemporary Northwest Women Photographers.

amy MULLEN

All work untitled

For Susan, the Palouse serves as the equivalent of Claude Monet's Giverney. Her paintings are like stories on canvas, of the landscape at work, with day-to-day and season-to-season changes that carry a network of meaning.

ARTIST'S STATEMENT

SUSAN POPE

Susan was born in Spokane, Washington, on the edge of the Palouse an area of northeast Washington and northern Idaho. She received a BA from Washington State University in Pullman in the heart of the area. In her youth she disliked the Palouse because "she could see for ever." However after many years of living an urban life she discovered that she in fact loved the Palouse for the same reason she had disliked it before, "she could see forever." In her paintings she explores its landscape, its vastness and the variety of its nature and its seasons. Susan teaches at the North Seattle Community College and her work is in numerous collections around the Northwest.

susan POPE

OPPOSITE PAGE: Swamp II, oil 40 x 30"
THIS PAGE: Wind Swept, oil 40 x 30"; Palouse, oil 40 x 30"

My work in this series is painted in oil on acrylic underpainting. I use tools and acrylic mediums to manipulate the acrylic surface in the early stages of the painting. Reference materials are used sparingly, but I think they can be useful in the beginning of a piece. I tend to abandon references altogether by the time I reach the middle of the painting. I like to stay loose during the process to make spontaneous changes.

ARTIST'S STATEMENT

AJ POWER

Born in Ogden, Utah, in 1971, I grew up competing in regional art competitions and shows. At Ohio University, I continued to paint while completing a Biology degree. In 1992 I contracted for life science professors, drawing scientific illustrations for publication in various academic journals. After graduation in 1995 I traveled extensively. I worked as a Peace Corps Volunteer in Gambia (West Africa) for two years and in Alaska as a Fisheries Observer in the Bering Sea for a year. In 2000, I moved to Seattle with the intent of building a career as an artist. In 2001 I served on the Immunex Corporate Arts board, compiling a new art collection but in 2002 I quit corporate work and began to work fulltime as a studio artist. Memories of my life's events shape the content of my work.

aj .POWER

opposite page: Lawol, oil 40 x 30¨
this page, clockwise from left: Little Herder, oil 40 x 30¨
Canary Island, oil 40 x 24¨; Doogugol #2, oil 40 x 30¨
Flycatchers, oil 40 x 30¨

this page: Mangos on the Way, oil 40 x 24″ **opposite page, from left:** Fatou's Baby #3, oil 40 x 24″
Jim Woodring's Toys, oil 40 x 24″; Bird over Precarious Landscape, oil 40 x 24″

My work is a form of painting comprised of pre-printed commercial cardboard boxes that have been fragmented and assembled into compositions of complexity and order. In the context of painting, found cardboard becomes a ready-made source of color. The material quality is contrary to traditional painting and remains to an extent non-archival. Its utilization is a poetic expression of the heightened regularity of obsolescence in contemporary life and a comment about 20th century art and art of today.

I have developed methods and a process; translating cardboard printed text, numbers, colors, barcodes and graphics to an art form. Lamination, fragmentation, inlay and collage are the methods I most commonly use to complete the translation. Compositions are built up by repetitively inlaying cut out shapes of varying sizes into a pre-assembled cardboard panel and integrating all fragments of material into a flat surface with minor sculptural relief.

My inspiration comes from quotes made by other artists about the infinity of painting and opposing arguments that painting is dead. Influenced by the New York Dadaists and Marcel Duchamp's ready-mades, I used objects on and beneath the surface of my paintings. Later, cardboard found on city streets, alleys, and parking lots became an interest in my experiments. I realized that cardboard found in printed form offered a fresh perspective of painting. I began using it exclusively and discovered new potentials within the material.

ARTIST'S STATEMENT

BRYAN SMITH

Bryan Smith is a graduate of Cornish College of the Arts, 2000. His major was in painting, sculpture and printmaking. Smith has been in solo and group shows in Seattle and is currently represented by Foster/White Gallery. He has been a featured artist at the Urban Institute of Contemporary Art in Grand Rapids, Michigan, and has work displayed in the Microsoft collection in Toronto, Canada. Smith lives and works in Seattle.

bryan SMITH

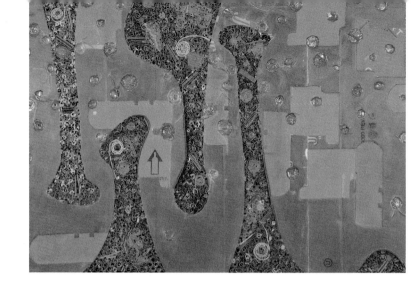

this page: Upside, mixed media 40 x 24" **opposite page:** Two Glass Pack, mixed media 40 x 24"; Bottles, mixed media 40 x 24"

"The man on the bus held a stuffed teddy bear in his arms. He talked to the bear for awhile, played with its two front paws as if it were a child, giggled and said I must be crazier than I thought."

When I began taking these images I was attracted to the physical surroundings. I was looking for, and finding, a certain film noir ambience that evoked qualities of suspense, drama and eeriness. I was drawn to the expressions of shadowy figures, their juxtaposition to inanimate objects, their behavior, and most of all to the appearance of isolation or alienation as I perceived it.

ARTIST'S STATEMENT

PAUL FORD

Paul Ford received an MA in Public Administration from the University of Akron, a Master of Science from Miami University and a BA in Political Science from Ohio Northern University. However photography was a passion that he has pursued with great enthusiasm. He studied fine art photography at the Photographic Center Northwest in Seattle and has taken part in a number of juried exhibitions, among them several shows at the Center and at the Bumbershoot Seattle Arts Festival in 2001. Among awards that he has received is the Maine Workshops 2004 Golden Light Top Photographers Award for Personal/Fine Art photography. The latest publication in which his work is featured is the *Penningtones CD, Amateur Status.* He finds a great deal of his inspiration on the streets of Paris.

paul FORD

top row, from left: Happy hands; Zorro; Lipstick; Pinko
bottom row: Rue Cremieux; Canal St. Martin; Heads

top row: Sax in the Metro; Look; Plats du Jour; Gare du Nord; Reclining
bottom row: Cross Purposes; Passage; Havana Skylight; Lingerie; Concorde

Working for the past eighteen years as a residential real estate appraiser, I have had the opportunity to see numerous homes in a variety of settings. While analyzing these residences with the left side of my brain, the right brain has noticed the link between the design and building choices we make and the effect on our lives, our spirit, and our community. These paintings reflect the memories and visions of the evolution and emotions I have experienced in my island community; they portray the conflict and integration of nature and architecture.

SHARON STRAUSS

Sharon was born in Dallas and as a young child lived abroad in cities as diverse as Rome, Johannesburg and Tokyo. Her earliest exposure to art and architecture was during this time and the artists she met there have remained a strong influence. Exposure to their creativity and passion instilled in her a curiosity that spurred her initial artistic experimentation. Sharon received a BA from the University of Northern Colorado and has exhibited widely in the Seattle area.

sharon STRAUSS

this page: Footprint, oil 40 x 24˝ **opposite page, from left:** Into the Woods, oil 40 x 30˝; When We Go Walking, oil 40 x 24˝; Blue Monday, oil 40 x 24˝

Painting for me is a process of discovery. I am very interested in the changing nature of landscape, and I seek out moments in my paintings that reflect that nature. color, activity, time and space can all trigger an intense engagement with a painting in me, and those connections are what keep me painting.

ARTIST'S STATEMENT

PEDER SUNDE

I was born in 1975 and spent my first few years in rural Duval, Washington. By the first grade my family was living in Seattle's University District. I graduated from the Bush School in 1993 where I had become serious about art. At age 18 I moved to Flagstaff, Arizona, to follow up on experiences that I had during high school at Big Mountain, a remote region of the Navajo Reservation. Over the next year I strengthened my relationships with the family that I came to know there, as well as the landscape. When I was given the opportunity to attend Cornish College of The Arts in 1994 I returned to Seattle, and received my BFA in 1999. Recently I spent six weeks as an artist in residence in Ollantaytambo, Peru. I am currently running my own small construction company and painting on the side.

peder SUNDE

opposite page: Outcropping, oil 40 x 30"
this page, clockwise from left: Vashon Spring, oil 40 x 30"
Near the River at Night, oil 40 x 30"; Afternoon Tide, oil
40 x 30"; Around the Bend, oil 40 x 30"

above: Untitled February, oil 40 x 30"

ADELE SYPESTEYN

Adele Sypesteyn was born and raised in New Orleans. Growing up in an artistic family, she was introduced to the arts at a young age. Her mother, who was also an artist, was her greatest mentor and earliest influence. She was very influenced by the architecture and the multilayered, aged walls of New Orleans and the exploration of subtle layers of color and texture, as seen in the old buildings, has remained a focus in her art. She earned a BA with a major in art history from Tulane University and later earned a master's degree in social work, also from Tulane University. She started to paint professionally 20 years ago when she joined the Evans Gallery in New Orleans. She moved to Seattle in 1997, where she continues to live and work. She is currently represented by eight galleries nationwide and is in many national collections.

I see my paintings as a form of archeology. An archeologist reveals the details of how a people lived by carefully removing layer after layer of dirt and artifacts from a site. Similarly, in my works patterns and other painted artifacts are offered to the viewer in layers. For me, my paintings evoke the slow, accumulated and interactive effects of weather, erosion and the visual marks of generations of peoples' lives playing themselves out on a wall.

ARTIST'S STATEMENT

adele SYPESTEYN

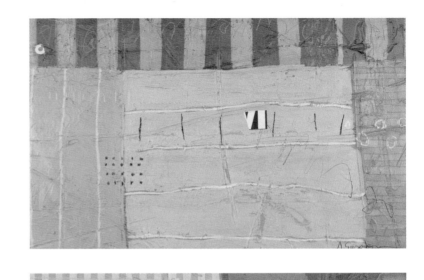

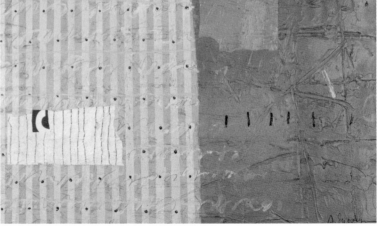

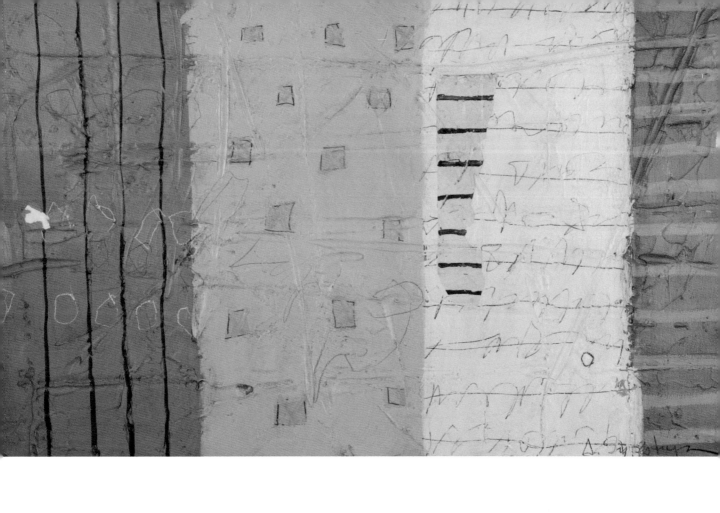

this page: Outrageous, mixed media 40 x 24¨ **opposite page:** Hurried Look, mixed media 40 x 24 ¨; Mostly There, mixed media 40 x 24¨

Great photographic opportunities occur all around us with scenes that are sad, humorous, ironic or just plain bizarre.
The photographer's challenge is to strip away any extraneous background revealing the essence and emotion of a scene.

JOHN ARMSTRONG

Born in Evanston, Illinois, in 1946, John Armstrong has been passionate about photography since he first learned basic photography and darkroom skills for a high school science project. After graduating from Iowa State, Michigan State and the University of Washington, John settled in Seattle. Since recently retiring as a scientist for the U.S. Environmental Protection Agency, John has dedicated much more of his time to photography.

Perhaps due to his early years in the Chicago area, John often photographs in urban areas. His photos depict the human condition: people, odd juxtapositions, windows, signs, irony and humor. John carries his camera with him everywhere and if he can't immediately take a photo he'll note the location and the light to return later.

While largely self-taught, John has taken several photography courses at Seattle's Photographic Center Northwest. John feels his work has been influenced by photographers Walker Evans and Robert Frank, among many others.

john ARMSTRONG

top row, from left: Dog House; Truck Tires; Fragile, Produce
bottom row: Psychic; Dog Sign; Fremont Bridge Espresso

top row: Sally Stitch; Windshield Surfer; Rue Reaumur, Paris; Dancing Neon Couple; Vertigo Building
bottom row: Turn Here; Welcome to Seattle; Bowling with Superman; Coffee, Tea, Ice Cream; Econotax

I have recently become interested in the idea of entropy, "a hypothetical tendency for the universe to attain a state of maximum homogeneity." In other words, everything is more or less coming apart. My desire to express this manifests itself in both my process which allows some chaos, and my images which hopefully do not sit still.

ARTIST'S STATEMENT

AMY WILLIAMS

Amy Marie Williams is a painter and a performance artist. After traveling the country and attending seven colleges, she received her BFA from University of Washington in 1987. Ten years and two children later, she went back to the UW for her MA. Amy exhibits her work in group and solo shows both locally and in national galleries. Credits include the Henry Art Gallery and COCA in Seattle and the Fraser Gallery in Washington, DC. She toured nationally with the performance group a.k.a and co-founded Here Now Productions. In addition to painting, performance, and teaching, Amy is also a writer. She has written and produced a play as well as published various essays and art criticism. She currently teaches art at the University of Washington, the Art Institute of Seattle and the Art Center on Bainbridge Island, a community art school co-founded by her.

WILLIAMS
amy

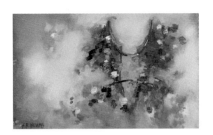

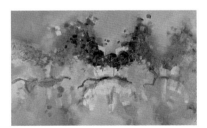

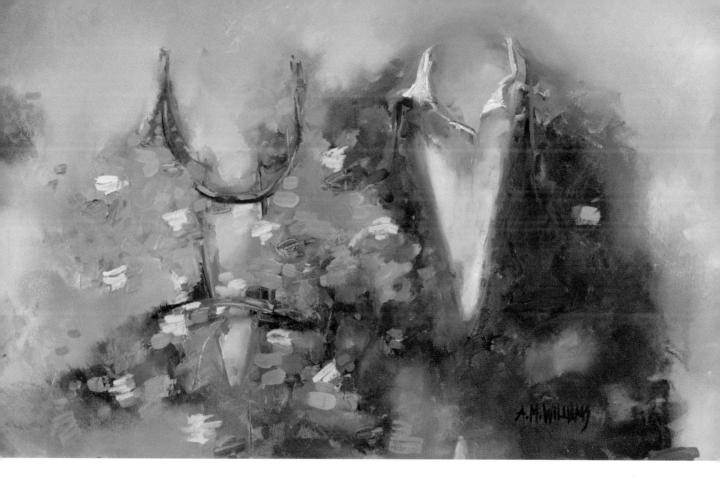

A.M.WILLIAMS

this page: Couple, oil 40 x 24¨ **opposite page. clockwise from left:** Dress, oil 40 x 24¨; Sticks, oil 40 x 24¨;Trio, oil 40 x 24¨; Sisters, oil 40 x 24¨; Dress for Degas, oil 40 x 24¨

Collaborating with my medium, I am always making discoveries. Working intuitively and quickly I pour onto a hard surface or onto watercolor paper on the floor. Fluid movements inform the piece as I apply objects and ink or diluted paint. I may peel away or add more layers, and wait. Leaving rubber bands, washers, paper or other objects on the surface for up to two days will create a hyper real, sharp line or removing them quickly will leave an amorphous bleed. Only through time is my work fully realized.

As I carve into a painting to reveal a previous layer I dive into unknown waters. I cannot see what is underneath and that is what really excites me, the elements of chance and exploration.

ARTIST'S STATEMENT

RICKIE WOLFE

Rickie Wolfe received her BFA from Cornish College of the Arts in Seattle, Washington in 2000. At Cornish she established herself as an alchemist and printmaker. "I always had to invent a new way to work." Rickie's work is shown and collected in the Northwest and nationally. She is in several public and private collections including the Lundy Collection in Houston, Texas, the Harrington-Smith in Aspen, Colorado and the Cornish College of the Arts Print Collection in Seattle, Washington. The Seattle Art Museum Rental/Sales Gallery represents Rickie in Seattle.

rickie WOLFE

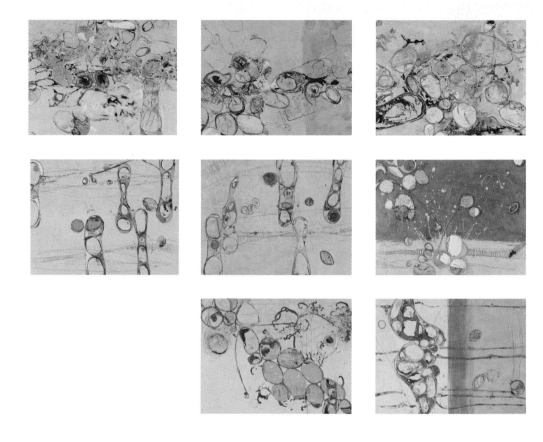

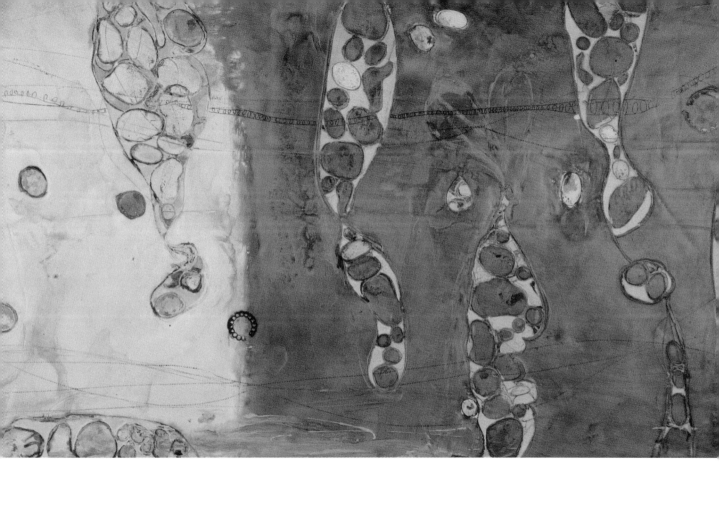

this page: Under the Big Tent IV, mixed media 40 x 24"

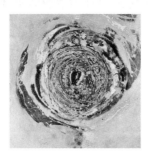

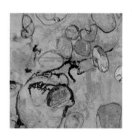

above, from left: Brown CIrcles, mixed media 28 x 28"
Crosswinds V, mixed media 30 x 30"
CIrcles, mixed media 12 x 12"

JUNKO YAMAMOTO

Photo:
Kaori Tanimoto

Junko was born in Tokyo, Japan, in 1973. She has drawn since the age of 3 and learned to paint at 6 years old. She came to USA alone for study at age of 16 and has lived in Seattle ever since. She graduated with a Bachelor of Fine Arts Degree Cum Laude from Cornish College of the Arts in 1999. She learned print making, sculpture and painting at Cornish. She has had solo exhibitions at King County Art Gallery, AT31 Gallery, Seattle, and has participated in group shows at the Bellevue Art Museum, the Seattle Art Museum Rental Sales gallery, the Kirkland Arts Center, Kirkland, WA, Gas Gallery, Torino, Italy, and RC-Gallery, Portland, Oregon. She feels that painting is such an isolated process, so working and communicating with people, connecting people to people and any hands on experiences inspires her more than reading any great book or information.

When we scale everything down to a subatomic level, we no longer see isolated particles, but we experience oneness: a field of dynamic energy. My latest work is based on my own thinking about the notion of Shunyata, to me it represents a belief that everything in our physical world is a temporary vessel filled with a universal consciousness. I wonder about expansion and the boundaries of knowledge, memory and possession where a sense of values and existence is not actually tangible. In my approach to creating these images, I strive to bring form to this seemingly ineffable experience.

junko YAMAMOTO

opposite page:
Shunyata Series/Memories (Change), oil 40 x 30"
this page, from left:
Shunyata Series/Memories (Glance), oil 40 x 30"
Shunyata Series/Memories (Possibility), oil 40 x 30"
Shunyata Series/Memories (Stream), oil 40 x 30"

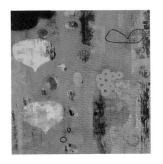
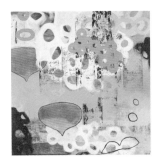

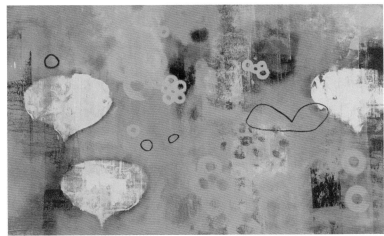

clockwise, from left:
Shunyata Series/Memories (Choose), oil 30 x 30˝; Shunyata
Series/Memories (Rain), oil 40 x 24˝; Shunyata Series/
Memories (Sense), oil 40 x 24˝; Shunyata Series/Memories
(Remember), oil 30 x 30˝

clockwise, from left:
Shunyata Series/Memories (Take), oil 30 x 30¨
Shunyata Series/Memories (Sway), oil 40 x 30¨
Shunyata Series/Memories (Connection), oil 40 x 30¨

LORI PATRICK

Lori Patrick is lucky to have a photograph featured on the most used door in the joint — the women's restroom. An amateur photographer, Lori earned a certificate in fine art photography from the University of Washington Extension. By day, she manages cultural programs for the City of Auburn, where she completed a photo essay on the Miss Auburn Pageant in 2003 and snapped the timeless image of pageant contestant Allison Miller featured in The Max Hotel. Lori likes to garden, bake, drink wine, commiserate with her twin sister and fix her 100-year-old West Seattle fixer-upper house with her husband, Geoff. Would you like a cracker with that Spackle?

lori PATRICK

WOMEN'S RESTROOM

A Girl from Aberdeen

charles PETERSON

MEN'S RESTROOM

The Boy from Aberdeen

I am integrating my feeling for both sculpture and painting through focusing on the unique qualities of distressed paper. Individual works often require over 100 ft. of paper prepared with ink and pigment that is then pressed into a mold to create the final effect.

DEBBIE YOUNG

I was born and raised in Ellensburg, Washington, and obtained my BA in Art and Anthropology from Central Washington University in 1981. I supported myself as a professional photographer and returned to fine art in 1996. After painting figuratively for 6 years I realized that working in two dimensions alone would not adequately express my experience and I followed the urge to work sculpturally with paper. I am interested in the creation of abstract line and form through the process of distressing paper as well as evoking a sense of place. My current work is a culmination of living in the foothills of the Cascade Mountains and reflects my intuitive relationship to the natural environment.

debbie YOUNG

opposite page: Stick Forest, mixed media 40 x 30¨
clockwise, from left: Rust, mixed media 39 x 28¨
Green, mixed media 37 x 20¨; Red, mixed media 37 x 28¨

P John Armstrong (10th Floor)
JJDArmstrong@msn.com
206.367.3030

Pam Baker
oiltrouble@hotmail.com

Jackie Barnett
JB4art@aol.com

P Roniq Bartenen (7th Floor)
www.roniqbartanen.com
206.229.7858

Pirjo Berg
www.alpineworks.com/berg
pirjoberg@hotmail.com

P Joan Broughton (3rd Floor)
jmbrou@earthlink.net

Andrée Carter
www.andreecarter.com
abstractAC@aol.com
206.412.5858

Eric Day Chamberlain
ericdayc@yahoo.com
206.522.5996

Layne Cook
www.laynecook.com
layne@laynecook.com
206.542.7336

Tony Evanko
tonyevanko@earthlink.net

P Paul Ford (9th Floor)
paul.ford@seattle.gov

Keven Furiya
www.furiya.com
kfuriya@gmail.com

Gretchen Gammell
elevengrets@yahoo.com

Gail Grinnell
www.gailgrinnell.com

Evy Halvorsen
blondeart7@aol.com
360.297.2828

Stephanie Hargrave
www.stephaniehargrave.com

Virginia Howlett
www.blueskyartist.com
virginia@blueskyartist.com
206.550.2192

P = PHOTOGRAPHER

Gaylen Iwasaki
gaylensho@yahoo.com
206.227.4636

Howard Jacobs
www.howardjacobs.com
howard@howardjacobs.com

Kamla Kakaria
kkakaria@pratt.org

Zanetka Kralova Gawronski
jupitersquirrel@hotmail.com
206.999.3553

Moon Lee
www.moonleeartstudio.com
moonleeartstudio@hotmail.com
425.746.8240

Kiki Macinnis
kikmac@comcast.net

Jo Moniz
www.monizfineartimages.com
jomoniz@maa.cc

Doris Mosler
www.dorismosler.com

(P) Amy Mullen (8th Floor)
amynmullen@earthlink.net

(P) Lori Patrick (Women's Restroom)
lori.patrick@comcast.net

(P) Charles Peterson (5th Floor)
charlesphoto@speakeasy.net

Susan Pope
www.suepope.com
sbpope@comcast.net
206.364.9395

(P) Zuzana Sadkova (6th Floor)
www.zuzanafoto.com
amina@email.cz

(P) Erin Shafkind (2nd Floor)
mustardworkstudio.com
mustardpie@mindspring.com

AJ Power Studio
patehpower@hotmail.com
206.818.3941

Bryan Smith
bryansmithvis@msn.com

Sharon Strauss
sharonkstrauss@hotmail.com

(P) Paul Sundberg (4th Floor)
paulsundberg@hotmail.com

CONTACT INFORMATION

Peder Sunde
jacksund@hotmail.com
360.715.8555

Adele Sypesteyn
www.adelesypesteyn.com

Amy Williams
amy@artconspiracy.net

Ricki Wolfe
rickiwolfe@msn.com

Junko Yamamoto
www.junkoyamamoto.com
junko@junkoyamamoto.com

Debbie Young
www.debbieyoungart.com
mail@debbieyoungart.com

Contact:
denise@corsostaicoff.com
503.231.9222

When designing the Hotel Max we were faced with many challenges. Small rooms, quirky bathrooms and "interesting" views. The design had to take the guests' attention away from the challenges and focus it toward a unique experience. Engaging the local Seattle art community to create the unique experience became the solution. They provided hundreds of quality original pieces of art. Edgy black and white photographs cover the guestroom entry doors and the room design is purposefully minimal in order to focus the attention on the paintings. No two rooms are alike because no two pieces of artwork are alike. Every visit is a new experience.

The Hotel Max is not only a hotel....it's a comfortable place to see original artwork and an interesting venue for emerging artists. I am thankful for all the artists and the project team: David Kennedy, Cara King, Elaine Chan and Tessa Papas who made the Hotel Max what it is — a maximum experience in a minimal space.

Denise Corso, Hotel Max Designer

Contact:
info@papasart.com
888.695.4226

Tessa Papas was born in England and showed an early talent for painting; at age 12 a watercolor of hers was accepted and hung in the Junior Royal Academy in London. However it was not until after her marriage to the Guardian cartoonist, Bill Papas, and their subsequent move to Greece in 1970 that she started to paint seriously. She has exhibited in Jerusalem, Geneva and frequently in Athens, Greece.

In 1984 She and Bill moved to Portland, Oregon, and for the next 15 years she owned and ran an art gallery. During this time they also wrote, illustrated and published a number of books including Papas' Portland *and* Papas' Greece. *Though the gallery allowed little time for Tessa to pursue her painting career it enabled her to learn the art business from the other side of the fence. She closed the gallery in 2003 and now finds herself uniquely qualified as an art consultant to the hotel and hospital trades. She has started to paint again and hopes to have a sufficient body of work to exhibit next year. The Hotel Max is the fourth hotel that she has been involved with.*